NATIVE AMERICAN MAZES

Winky Adam

DOVER PUBLICATIONS, INC.
Mineola, New York

Bibliographical Note

Native American Mazes is a new work, first published by Dover
Publications, Inc., in 2003.

International Standard Book Number

ISBN-13: 978-0-486-42616-7
ISBN-10: 0-486-42616-5

Manufactured in the United States of America
4 2 6 1 6 5 0 4
www.doverpublications.com

Note

This little book will teach you about Native American life as you complete 33 challenging mazes. You will learn the names of many different tribes and read about types of Native American homes and objects or activities associated with Native Americans, such as sand painting, Kachina dolls, the potlatch, and lacrosse. Try to finish all of the mazes on your own. There is a Solutions section on pages 52 through 63 just in case you need help. When you have finished doing the mazes, you can have even more fun by coloring them with crayons or colored pencils. Enjoy!

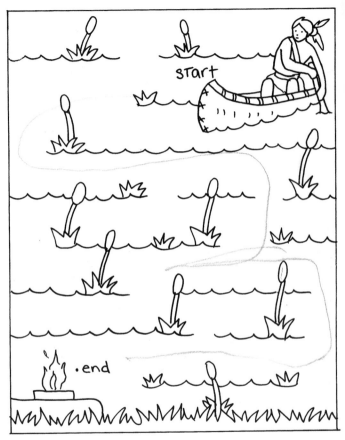

start

.end

Help this young Pequot paddle his birchbark canoe across the river to his campfire.

4

One of the three Mimbres [**mim** bris] designs goes on the bowl. Do the maze to find out which design belongs.

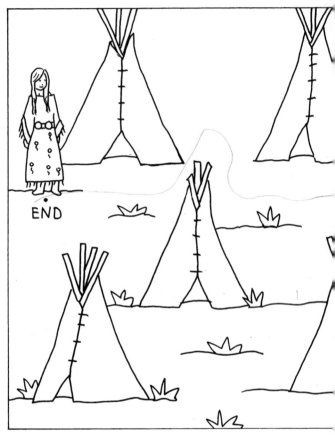

END

This Sioux [soo] girl is on her way home to help her mother. Show her the correct path through the teepees.

6

START

START

Help the light from the rising sun find its way to the front door of the Navajo *hogan* (house).

8

•END

9

END.

Help this Seminole woman find her way through the Everglades swamp to her home, called a *chickee*.

10

START

The corn in this Hopi field is waiting for the rain.
Help the rain cloud find its way to the corn.

12

The Haida [**high** duh] boy wants to ask the half-animal, half-human mask for a favor. Help him find the way.

END

START

Help the Navajo man reach the sand painting so that its healing powers can make him feel better.

14

The Southwestern Mimbres quail wants to meet its lizard friend at the end of the path. Help it get there.

START

Help the Naskapi [**nass** kuh pea] hunter on snow-shoes find the way through the forest to his teepee.

16

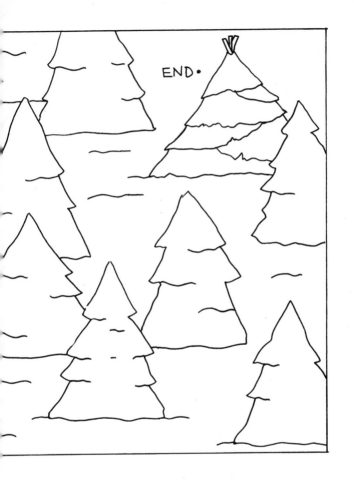

END.

START

This Inuit hunter needs to get through the ice to his
igloo. Choose the correct path for him.

18

END.

A Haida boy is on his way to visit his cousin. Help him choose the correct path.

START

END

START

The Hopi boy is looking for his Kachina doll. Can you help him get to it?

22

The Nez Perce used decoys—wooden ducks—to attract real ducks. Help the real duck find the decoy.

Help this mouse find its way home through the Iroquois "three sisters"—pumpkins (squash), corn, and beans.

24

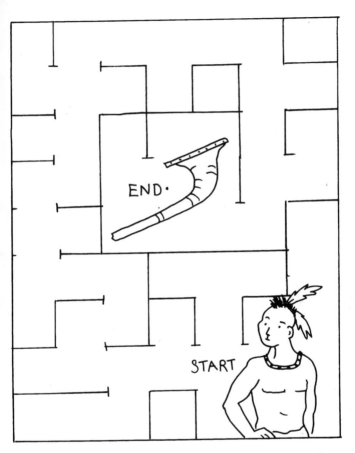

This Mohawk warrior is going to an important meeting.
Help him get his peace pipe to take along.

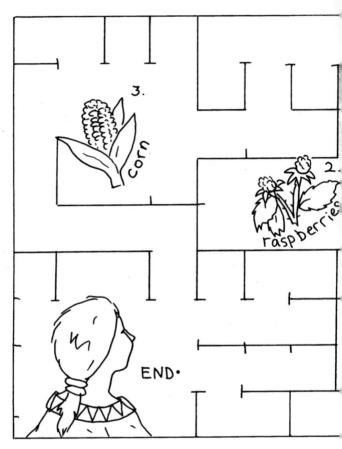

A Seneca man is gathering dinner for his waiting wife. Show him the way to get to the end.

26

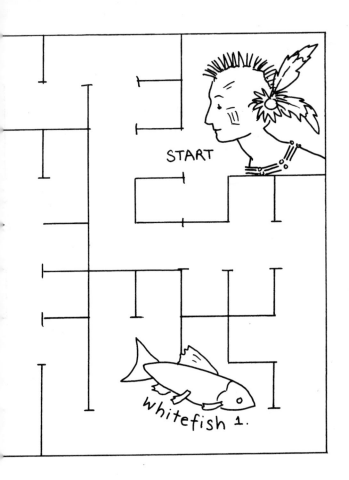

START

whitefish 1.

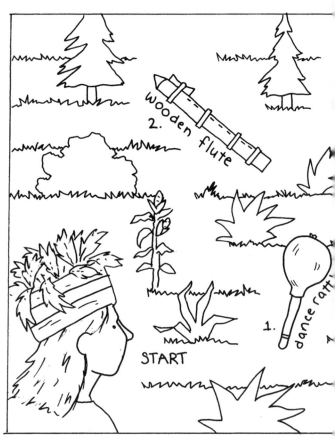

Help the Cherokee musician pick up his instruments as he follows the path to his home.

END.

drum
3.

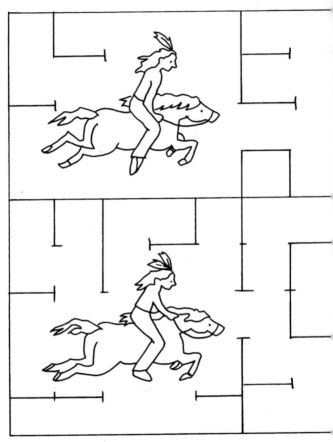

Which Sioux warrior will win the race? Follow the maze to find out.

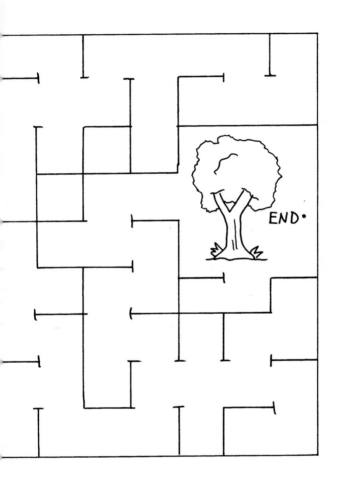

END.

31

START

The game of lacrosse was created by Native Americans. Do the maze to find out which player will catch the ball.

32

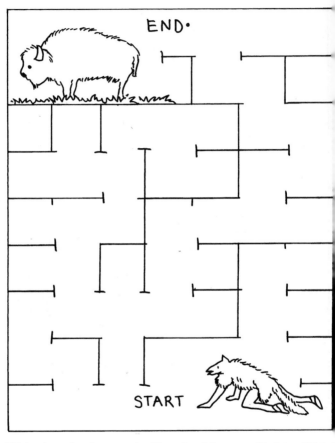

This Apache hunter is disguised in a wolf skin. Help him sneak up on the buffalo by showing him the path.

This Sioux horse is hitched to a carrier called a *travois* [truh **voy**]. Help the horse drag its load to the teepee.

35

START

Northwest Coast chiefs gave gifts at *potlatch* feasts. Help this Chilkat chief give away an engraved copper plate.

•END

37

Show this Chippewa fisherman the correct path to use to paddle home to his wigwam.

38

The Zuni woman needs to reach the painted pot at the end of the path. Help her get to it.

START

• END

Help the Apache girl find her woven basket. Show her the correct path.

40

This bird's eye view shows Iroquois longhouses. Help the boy find the way to his waiting friend.

41

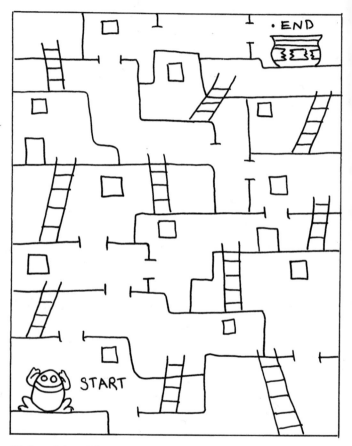

Help this thirsty frog find its way through the Anasazi cliff dwelling to the bowl of water.

This Arapaho boy wants to play with his toy horse. Help him get to it.

Plains Indians sent messages over great distances using smoke signals. Help this Apache man get a message to his friend.

44

START

START

• EN

This Iroquois man needs to get his False Face mask from the longhouse. Show him the correct path.

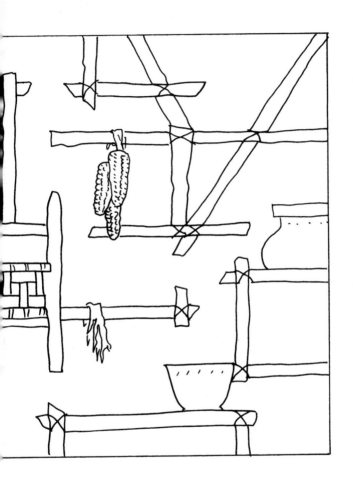

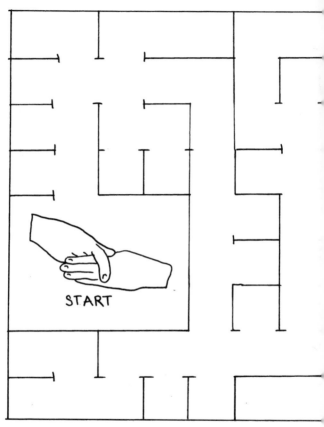

Great Plains tribes spoke different languages, but they understood hand signals. Do the maze to learn the meaning of this signal.

48

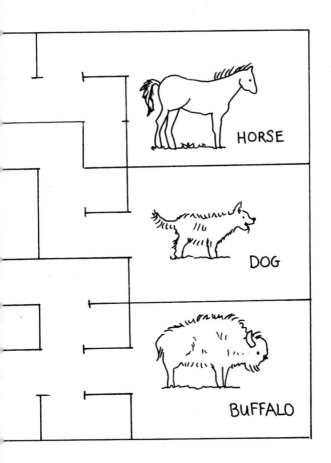

HORSE

DOG

BUFFALO

START

Help the stag get past the Narragansett hunter and meet its friend at the end of the trail.

50

END

51

Solutions

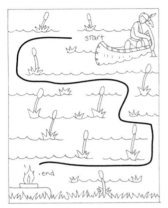

Page 4

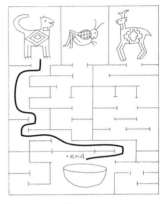

Page 5

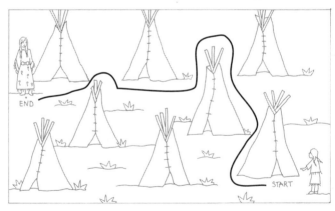

Pages 6-7

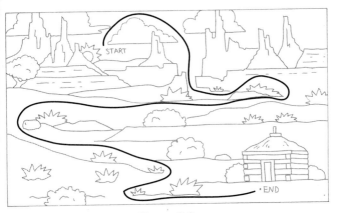

Pages 8-9

Pages 10-11

Page 12

Page 13

Page 14

Page 15

54

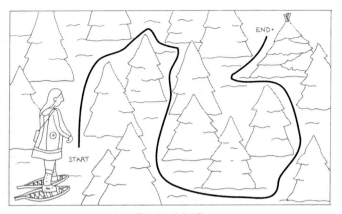

Pages 16-17

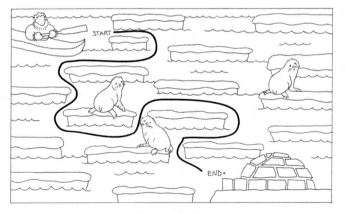

Pages 18-19

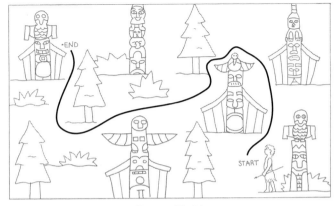

Pages 20-21

Page 22

Page 23

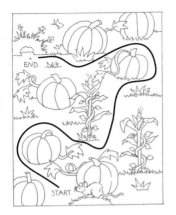

Page 24

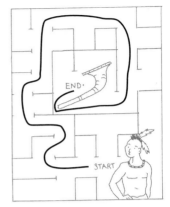

Page 25

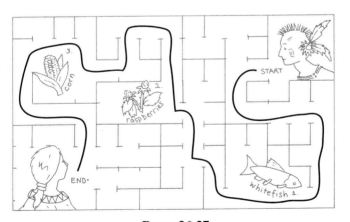

Pages 26-27

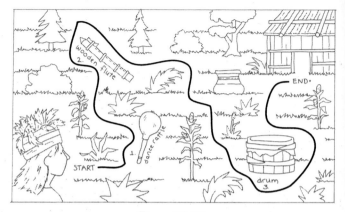

Pages 28-29

Pages 30-31

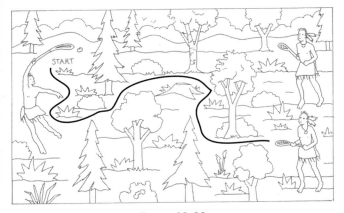

Pages 32-33

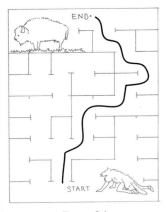

Page 34

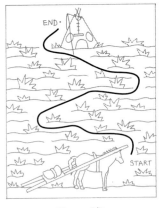

Page 35

Pages 36-37

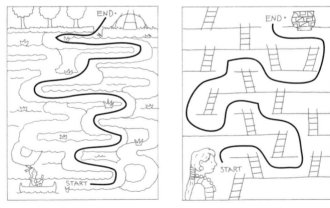

Page 38

Page 39

Page 40

Page 41

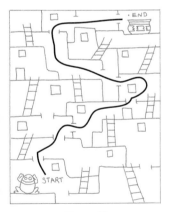

Page 42

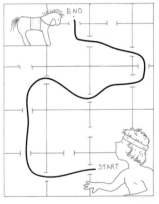

Page 43

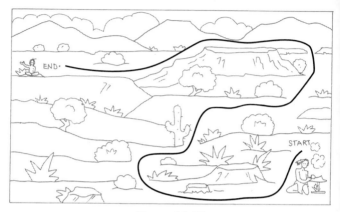

Pages 44-45

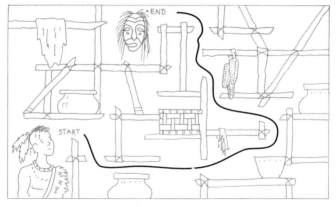

Pages 46-47

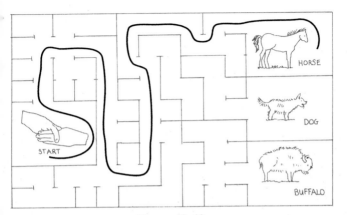

Pages 48-49

Pages 50-51